CONTENTS

Gaúcho, p.19

Poison dart frog, p.27

WHAT'S HOT: BRAZIL

Visiting Brazil is a rollercoaster ride of **extremes:** rich and poor, grassland and rainforest, beaches and mountains, cities and countryside. There's so much to see that it's hard to know where to start. Here are a few ideas:

Bonete Beach, p.32

Amazon surfing, p.22

1. HAVE A SNACK AT COPACABANA p.12

Enjoying the sun and sea at Brazil's most famous beach can be hungry work. Stop at one of the kiosks for a portion of fried sausage and lime juice!

2. WATCH THE *CLASSICO MAJESTICO* p.28

Football is a bit like a religion in Brazil. In São Paulo, the fans get really worked up for the *Classico Majestico* match, the old rivalry between the city's two biggest teams.

3. TAKE PART IN A COWBOY COOKOUT p.18

There are hundreds of mouth-watering foods in Brazil, from fresh seafood to cakes. But at the top of many people's list is *churrasco* – cowboy barbecue, Brazilian style.

4. CATCH A WAVE IN THE AMAZON p.22

It seems a bit unlikely, but one of the world's strangest surfing contests takes place each year at São Domingos do Capim, 300 km from the ocean.

Bumba meu boi festival, p.38

5. GO FISHING FOR PIRANHA p.24

The 'most ferocious fish in the world' turns out to be not QUITE as fearsome as its reputation suggests – but catching and eating one is still an exciting experience!

6. LEARN TO SAMBA p.36

Samba is Brazil's most famous dance. There are schools everywhere that will teach you the basics

– but Rio de Janeiro, the home of samba, is a great place to learn a dance that has spread from Brazil to just about every other country in the world.

7. PARTY AT BUMBA MEU BOI p.38

In late July and August, the town of São Luis is taken over by one of Brazil's craziest festivals, with performers dressed as oxen and fantastical creatures wandering the streets.

IT'S (NEARLY) OFFICIAL!
TOP PLACES TO VISIT IN BRAZIL

Members of one of the world's biggest travel websites picked these top Brazilian destinations:

1. Rio de Janeiro – the beaches, the architecture and the landscape of the city all pull in millions of visitors each year.

2. Florianópolis – a modern city on an island ringed by beautiful beaches, with great seafood and countryside: what's not to like?

3. São Paulo – Brazil's biggest city is football-crazy (like the rest of the country): head for the Museum of Football to find out more.

4. Búzio – the capital of Brazil's beach life, Búzio has something for everyone who loves the ocean, from

surfers to snorkellers and sailors.

5. Salvador – sometimes known as 'the capital of joy' because of the amazing carnival celebrations held here every year.

6. Foz do Iguaçu – exploring the waterfalls on the border between Brazil and Argentina is a highlight of any trip to southern Brazil and can be done in a raft or on foot.

7. Paraty – an old colonial town on the coast, Paraty's pedestrian-only streets are a great place for imagining what Brazil must have been like 150 years ago.

BRAZIL FACTS AND STATS

B razil is an amazing, breathtaking place to visit. It is a land of contrasts and surprises. There are steamy rainforests and snow-capped mountains; amazing modern buildings and terrible favela slums; beautiful beaches and the bare earth of stripped-away forest.

LANDSCAPE

As you'd expect from the largest country in South America, Brazil has a wonderful variety of landscapes. Highlights to watch out for include:

* The amazing Amazon River, which in places is 10 km or more wide, carries 20% of all the river water to reach the world's oceans

* Serra de Bocaina, a national park popular with people who love the outdoors, which includes beautiful forests and the mountain known as *Pico do Tira do Chapéu* (Hat-Off Peak)

* The Devil's Throat, one of the waterfalls that make up Iguaçu Falls on the border with Argentina

* The isolated islands of Fernando de Noronha, far out in the Atlantic Ocean, which are especially popular with divers and snorkellers

Key
■ Capital city
○ Other cities

COLOMBIA
VENEZUELA
GUYANA
FRENCH GUIANA
SURINAME
North Atlantic Ocean
Rio Negro
Manaus
Amazon River
A M A Z O N
Tocantins River
NORTH-EAST
PERU
B R A Z I L
CENTRE-WEST
BOLIVIA
PANTANAL
■ Brasília
PLANALTO
South Atlantic Ocean
SOUTH-EAST
São Paulo
Rio de Janeiro
Santos
CHILE
PARAGUAY
Pacific Ocean
ARGENTINA
SOUTH
URUGUAY

N
W   E
S

miles   500
0
0   500
kilometres

Map of Brazil

CLIMATE

Brazil is just a little smaller than the USA. Like the USA it has variations in its climate, though they are not as extreme.

In most of Brazil the climate is tropical, with hot or warm weather throughout the year and frequent rain during the wet season. Usually shorts, a T-shirt and flip-flops are comfortable (Brazilians do sometimes like to dress up a bit more than this!). In winter, a light jacket or a sweater might be needed at night.

Far to the south, the weather is temperate: still mostly warm, but with noticeable seasons. Where there are higher mountains, in the south and southeast, the temperature is cooler higher up.

They call it 'rainforest' for a reason

Beach dance party

FACT FILE ONE

CAPITAL CITY: Brasília

AREA: 8,459,417 km² (land territory), plus 55,460 km2 (ocean territory)

HIGHEST POINT: Pico da Neblina (2994 m)

LOWEST POINT: Atlantic Ocean (0 m)

LONGEST RIVER: Amazon (6,400 km)

BORDERS: Argentina, Bolivia, Colombia, French Guiana, Guyana, Paraguay, Peru, Suriname, Uruguay, Venezuela.

NATURAL HAZARDS: droughts in the northeast; floods and sometimes frosts in the south

PEOPLE

The first settlers in Brazil were Amerindians. They are the descendants of people who tens of thousands of years ago crossed a bridge of land, which has since disappeared, between Asia and North America.

Carnival crowd, Rio

A young Amerindian, Brazilian Amazon

BRAZILIANS TODAY

In the early 1500s, Europeans began crossing the Atlantic and settling in Brazil. Brazil was claimed by Portugal and Brazilians still speak Portuguese today. Many Amerindians were forced into slavery and soon began to die of mistreatment or European diseases. Then, black people were brought from Africa to replace them.

Today, there are still some Amerindians. Most Brazilians, though, are descended from either Portuguese settlers or black Africans. Other large groups of immigrants have come to Brazil from Italy, Germany, Spain, Japan and Lebanon.

RICH AND POOR

Brazil is a wonderful country, but it does have problems. One of the biggest is that although there is a lot of wealth in Brazil, many people – both in cities and the countryside – are very poor. It's not unusual to see children sleeping in the streets, without a family to look after them. Even young people who do have families often live in badly built houses, rarely have good educations, and find it hard to get well-paid work. In cities such as Rio de Janeiro and São Paulo, this poverty is linked to serious street crimes, including mugging and even murder.

A favela (low-quality housing) in Rio de Janeiro

4 FAMOUS BRAZILIANS

Pelé – footballing legend and a national hero. Pelé now works to improve the conditions of poor Brazilians.

Ayrton Senna – one of the world's most charismatic sportspeople and six-times winner of the Monaco Grand Prix, Senna was killed in a racing accident in 1994.

Gisele Bundchen – one of the world's top models, famous for her typically Brazilian love of the beach. Gisele is also known for her charity and campaigning work.

Oscar Niemeyer – an architect who designed some of the most famous buildings of the twentieth century, including the key public buildings of Brasília.

FACT FILE TWO

POPULATION: 201 million

CITY POPULATION: São Paulo (20 million), Rio de Janeiro (12 million), Belo Horizonte (5.7 million), Porto Alegre (4 million), Brasília (3.8 million)

AGE STRUCTURE: 24.2% under 15 years old; 68.5% 15–64 years old; 7.3% over 64 years old

YOUTH UNEMPLOYMENT (15–24 year-olds): 17.8%

OBESITY: 11.1%

LANGUAGES: Portuguese is the official language and by far the most widely spoken. Small numbers of people also speak Spanish, German, Italian, Japanese and English

MAIN RELIGIONS: Christian (89%): 73.6% of Brazilians are Roman Catholic

RIO – DAY 1

Rio de Janeiro has always been Brazil's most popular city for foreign visitors. They come for the great beaches, nightlife, cafés, restaurants, shops and markets. But the biggest attraction is probably the city itself, with its steep hills, amazing architecture and incredible location among the hills beside the Atlantic Ocean.

Copacabana, Rio's most famous beach

A TRIP TO COPACABANA BEACH

Rio is a long flight away for many visitors from abroad. What better way to freshen up when you arrive than a trip to the beach? And if you're going to the beach, it might as well be one of the world's most famous: Copacabana!

Once you hit the beach you'll find plenty to do: sunbathing and swimming, of course, plus beach football, snacking or having a drink at the famous beach kiosks, people watching and listening to music.*

*Trivia fact: Copacabana is where the largest-ever music concert took place, in 1994, when Rod Stewart played at the New Year's Eve party.

CITY OF SPORT

Brazilians love sport (especially football: see page 28). So when it was announced that the city would be hosting the 2014 World Cup AND the 2016 Olympic Games, the people of Rio must have thought they were in heaven – though many also questioned the cost.

Celebrating the award of hosting the 2016 Olympic Games

NEW YEAR'S EVE

Every New Year, Copacabana hosts one of the biggest celebrations in the world. Over two million people crowd into the area for an all-night party and firework display.

Those spending New Year's Eve at the beach usually dress in white to bring good luck into the new year. Eating grapes or lentils is also associated with the holiday.

KIOSK CULTURE

Kiosks (in Portuguese, *quiosque*) are huts where you can buy drinks and food. Here are three insider tips for top Copacabana kiosks:

Skol: stop here for a portion of fried sausage and lime, washed down with fresh coconut milk

Trés: sells French food such as crêpes, as well as pasta and superb sandwiches

Maré e Mansa: once in a while a DJ party starts up here unannounced, so it's a lively spot for music lovers

Refreshment kiosk on Copacabana beach

RIO – DAY 2

Cable car view from Sugarloaf Mountain

Not far from Copacabana is Pão de Açúcar or Sugarloaf Mountain. This is part of a line of hills separating the beach side of Rio from the inland districts. Sugarloaf is a great place to visit as a way of getting your bearings: on a clear day you can see along the coast to both sides of the city.

"The friendliness of the cariocas (people born in Rio) can be witnessed in the streets... and at the beach, where the sunset is a rare experience."

— from the Rio Olympic Committee website

VISIT TO SUGARLOAF MOUNTAIN

Getting to Sugarloaf is a bit of an adventure, especially if you're not keen on heights. Many people will tell you that the best time to visit is to arrive just before sunset. Then you can stay as the city grows dark and watch the lights come on across Rio. If you're planning to do this, leave plenty of time – there are often queues:

Step 1: Catch the first cable car

Head for Praia Vermelha, where you can catch a cable car to Morro da Urca. (At the cable-car station, check out the ice-cream parlour Sorvete Brasil: it's one of the best in the city.)

Step 2: Catch the second cable car

From Morro da Urca, a second cable car whisks you upward for another three-minute ride, to Sugarloaf Mountain. Top tip: try to get a space at the rear of the car, for amazing views back towards Rio.

Step 3: Find somewhere to sit

There are restaurants and cafés at the top, though you'll have to buy a drink or some food to be allowed to sit down. There are also public benches where you can sit and soak in the views of Rio coming alight as the sun goes down.*

* **Locals' tip:** Watch out that the wild monkeys don't snatch your food/sunglasses/mobile etc: you'll never get them back!

Photographing a famous view, cable-car station, Rio

CHRIST REDEEMER

Perched on top of the Corcovado Mountain, looking down on Rio, is the Christ Redeemer statue. The statue is a symbol of Brazilian Christianity, and was finished in 1931. It is 30 metres tall, and made from concrete and soapstone.

Christ the Redeemer looks down on Rio de Janeiro

EATING IN BRAZIL

Most Brazilians eat three meals a day. Few people eat a big breakfast. Normally they just have a milky coffee, with either bread and butter, a grilled sandwich, cereal or fruit. Lunch (the main meal of the day for most people) and dinner (which is barely smaller than lunch) are larger meals. Some of these Brazilian favourites could feature in either meal:

Acarajé

SOUTH: *BARREADO*

Barreado probably originally came from the Azores, Portuguese islands off the coast of Africa. It's a shredded-beef stew, slow-cooked in a clay pot for 20 hours, served with rice and banana.

AMAZON: *TACACÁ*

This is a super-hot cassava-prawn stew. Fortunately it's made with jambu, a local plant that makes your mouth go numb – which you need, because this dish is SO HOT!

BAHIA: *ACARAJÉ*

Acarajé originated in West Africa, where food is often mouth-scorchingly spicy. It's a deep-fried cake of black-eyed peas, which is cut in half and filled with spiced prawns, cashew and other flavourings. YUM!

EVERYWHERE: *BRIGADEIRO*

Brazilian kids everywhere love Brigadeiro, a chocolate sweet a bit like a truffle. It often makes an appearance at birthday parties.

EVERYWHERE: *FEIJOADA*

Feijoada is often said to be Brazil's national dish. It's a black bean stew made with some sort of pork or beef (anything from pig's trotters or beef tongue to sausage). Feijoada is traditionally cooked in a clay pot, over a fire.

Eating is a social event in Brazil, and families try to get together for meals. It's very unusual and quite an honour for a visitor to be invited to a family meal – it means you have been accepted as a close friend.

TOP STREET FOOD

Brazilians love to stop for a bite of street food, and there are almost always sellers in busy spots. Sometimes, like the acarajé sellers in their white outfits (opposite), they even have a kind of semi-uniform. Here are a few top treats to look out for:

Queijo coalho: a kebab of cheese, cooked over a bucket of hot coals, which is nicer than it sounds

Espetinho de camarao: fresh prawns grilled or fried on a kebab stick, often served with lime juice

Pastel de feira: basically a massive deep-fried dumpling; the pastel stalls are usually run by Japanese-Brazilians

Empadinha: meat (e.g. prawn or chicken) and vegetables (e.g. palm hearts) packed into a pastry wrap. It's the Brazilian version of a Cornish pasty!

AND YOU PROBABLY WON'T WANT TO TRY...

Buchada: which is made from a billy goat's internal organs...

CHURRASCO – TOTAL BARBECUE

Loaded skewers

Food is almost always a social event in Brazil – and never more than at a churrasco, or barbecue. But if you're used to a 'barbecue' being your dad burning a few sausages out in the garden, a Brazilian churrasco will come as a pleasant surprise.

THE MEAL FROM COWBOY COUNTRY

The churrasco originally comes from the southern part of Brazil, particularly the state of Rio Grande. This is cowboy – or in southern Brazil, *gaúcho* – country. Everyone who eats churrasco is getting in touch with their inner gaúcho.

The gaúchos cooked salted meat on skewers, over a fire pit dug into the ground. This slow way of cooking the meat makes it incredibly tasty. Today, many southern Brazilian homes have a specially built churrasco area. There are also restaurants called *churrascaria* all over Brazil, where the meat is grilled over hot charcoal or wood embers. Waiters wander around with skewers of cooked meat, slicing helpings on to your plate. Churrascaria are usually all-you-can-eat – they keep bringing you more until you surrender.

Slicing meat at a churrascaria

SIDE DISHES AND DESSERTS

Churrasco is not an event for vegetarians – it's ALL about eating a lot of meat. But there are other dishes available on the side:

Farofa, a very popular Brazilian side dish a bit like couscous, made of manioc flour roasted with salt, smoked meat and spices

Salads include tomato and palm heart, carrot and chayote (a kind of squash that's used a bit like avocado), and onion salad

For dessert – if you have room – you might get a *pudim de leite* (creamy flan a teeny bit like crème caramel) or *torta de banana* (Brazilian banana pie)

"[We] made a great fire, cut the meat into long pieces about as thick as a finger tip, and then skewered them with a two-foot long rod. [We] cooked] one side, then the other."

— Augustin Saint-Hilaire, a French naturalist who explored Brazil, 1821

SALTING MEAT, GAÚCHO STYLE

In the past, gaúchos were said to have salted their churrasco meat in a surprising – and possibly slightly revolting – way. They put slices of meat under their saddles in the morning, and by evening the meat had been salted by the horse's sweat.

A gaúcho herds cattle in the Panatanal region

MARKET SHOPPING

The *feira*, or market, is a feature of Brazilian life. The local feira is the best place to get fresh fruit and vegetables. Other feira deal in specialist kinds of goods, for example fashion clothing or musical instruments, and draw customers from further away.

Street market in Ipanema

HAGGLING

Market stall holders selling clothes and other goods in Brazil can be open to a bit of haggling, where you try to persuade them to accept a lower price.

If you do decide to haggle, keep it good-natured, and remember that some Brazilians are very poor. A tiny amount extra to you might make a big difference to them.

Manaus city market

Night-time stalls at the Babilônia Feira Hype

VISITING BABILÔNIA FEIRA HYPE

If you're in Rio at the weekend, be sure to visit the Babilônia Feira Hype. Since it first started in 1996, this has become an institution among the city's young people. It's held at the weekend, at the Jockey Club in the Gávea district. The Feira Hype is a chance for the hottest new artists and designers to sell their products: well-known Brazilian brands such as Farm and Via Mia got their start here.

You'll see thousands of stalls selling clothes, jewellery, art, sunglasses, flip-flops – basically, everything a young hipster needs. Alongside the designers are the stalls of fortune tellers, henna tattooists and food sellers. There's also usually some live music being performed by a local band hoping for a break, which gives the whole place a lively atmosphere.

FOUR TOP MARKETS

MANAUS:
the famous Mercado Municipal Adolpho Lisboa is a cast-iron copy of Les Halles market in Paris. It has a distinctly Amazonian flavour, though: you can't buy Amerindian medicines in Les Halles, for example!

MINAS GERAIS:
visitors come here to see the famous flower and food markets.

BELO HORIZONTE:
the Sunday street fair is famous for clothes, jewellery, street food and MASSIVE crowds.

SÃO PAULO:
the Mercado Municipal is a beautiful building of stained glass and huge domes in the roof. Shop for fresh and dried food or try a mortadella sandwich, one of the local treats.

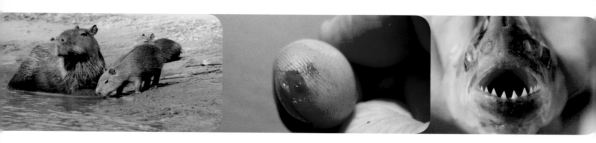

THE AMAZON

Swimming in the Tapajos River, Amazon region

Every day, enough water flows from the Amazon to provide New York City with water for 10 years. The forest here produces 20% of the world's oxygen, and is home to hundreds of thousands of species of birds, plants and animals. This place is a must-visit if you're coming to Brazil.

SURFING IN THE AMAZON

It's a long way from the ocean, but it's possible to surf in the Amazon. The wave is called *pororoca*, and is caused by tides at the river's mouth – though the pororoca can travel up to 800 km upriver.

In March and April, the town of São Domingos do Capim holds a contest to see who can ride the pororoca furthest and longest. The longest recorded ride on the wave lasted for 37 minutes.

AMAZON ATTRACTIONS

Of course, there is more to the Amazon than rainforest, river, rare animals and Amerindians. Those things are all there – but there's a lot else besides. These are locals' tips for an Amazon visit with a difference:

MAMIRAUÁ FLOODED FOREST

The Mamirauá national park is often said to be the most beautiful part of the Amazon. You can stay at a floating hotel, then paddle a canoe into the flooded forest. There are also marked walking trails to explore.

MANAUS

At first Manaus seems a crazy place – a huge city in the middle of the rainforest, with skyscrapers, grand theatres and an opera house built from European bricks, French glass, and Italian marble. In fact, it's a bustling city with plenty to see. One highlight is a trip to where the brown water of the Amazon and the black water of the Negro River meet.

THE CARIBBEAN OF THE JUNGLE

From the coastal city of Belém, catch a ferry up the river to Santarém. From here catch another boat to Alter de Chão. Nearby you'll find the most amazing white sandy beaches at the side of the river. It's easy to see how this area got the nickname 'Caribbean of the Jungle'. Close by is a national park with acres of natural rainforest to explore.

FISHING FOR PIRANHA

What could be more exciting than fishing for piranha, the deadly fish that can strip a body of its flesh in minutes? Actually, that's not EXACTLY true (see panel) – but they can give a nasty bite and you can go fishing for them. So, how would you go about it?*

* Note from the editor: We're not really suggesting you do this – and if you do, the Publisher accepts no responsibility for lost fingers.

Sharp little piranha teeth

STRIPPING A BODY IN SECONDS

The idea that a school of piranha can strip a body in seconds appeared in 1913. When US President Theodore Roosevelt visited Brazil, he saw a cow ripped to pieces by a school of piranha. What he DIDN'T know was that the fish had been deliberately starved for days beforehand.

Finger bitten by piranha

"They are the most ferocious fish in the world. Even... sharks or barracudas usually attack things smaller than themselves. But the piranhas habitually attack things much larger than themselves."

— US President Theodore Roosevelt, in *Through the Brazilian Wilderness*, 1914

1. FIND SOME PIRANHA

Really you want to catch the fiercest fish, green or pike piranha. These can be found in the following places:

- **green piranha:** the Rio São Francisco and its tributaries
- **pike piranha:** throughout the Amazon in the fast-flowing channels of bigger rivers, flooded forest areas and lakes.

2. CATCH SOME PIRANHA

Piranhas are pretty easy to catch if they're hungry (which they generally are). Just bait a hook with some meat and put it in the river. Attach the hook to a wire, rather than straight to the fishing line – otherwise the piranha will just bite through the line.

Piranha trivia: some species show their annoyance at getting caught by making a growling noise; their eyes also sometimes turn red.

3. COOK AND EAT YOUR PIRANHA

Piranhas are tasty once caught, and people in the Amazon use them as food. The most satisfying way to eat them is fresh roasted over a fire, or quickly fried with a squeeze of lime juice.

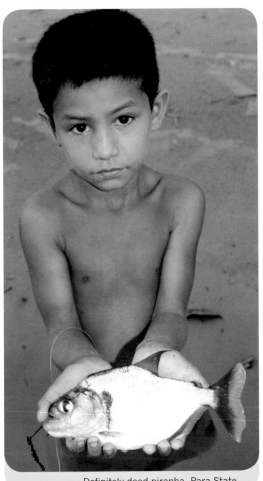

Definitely dead piranha, Para State

EVEN DEAD ONES ATTACK!

Even dead, cooked piranhas can do you harm. They have lots of tiny little forked bones, which can get stuck in the back of your throat. The locals eat piranha with their fingers: that way they can feel for the bones.

FREAKY FISHING

Other freaky fish you could try to catch in the Amazon:
- Payara – also called the Vampire Fish, because of its two huge, spiky lower teeth;
- Traiarao – sometimes called the Wolf Fish, very aggressive and with very sharp teeth;
- Aruana – its nickname, Monkey Fish, comes from its habit of jumping at low-hanging branches to catch birds, insects, snakes and lizards.

ENVIRONMENT

TOUR OF THE RAINFOREST CANOPY

Rainforest walkway

The trouble with exploring the rainforest is that for the most part, it's very, VERY thick. It's possible to cut paths, of course, but that's slow and hard work. Instead of slogging it out at ground level, why not head up into the canopy and get a bird's eye view?

TOUR OF THE TREE CANOPY

The canopy – the roof of the rainforest, the thick top layer of trees – can be 30–40 metres high. Don't try one of these tours if you are scared of heights! After climbing up, guides take you along narrow walkways and zip lines. You get to explore the rainforest like some kind of X-Men superhero. While you're up in the canopy you can spy on wildlife that doesn't even know you're there.

Animals to watch out for include capybaras, if you are anywhere near water: these are the world's biggest rodents. You may also see toucans, with their huge, brightly coloured bills, and all sorts of monkeys. With incredible luck, you could even get a glimpse of the rare cats of the forest, the jaguar and the ocelot.

Capybaras

AMAZON FACT FILE

- The Amazon region occupies almost half of South America and is the world's largest river basin

- Tropical rainforests contain roughly half of all the world's species. The Amazon contains one third of the world's tropical rainforests

- Amazon forest is currently being cut down at the rate of three football pitches every 60 seconds

ANIMALS TO AVOID

It really pays to watch out for these: not only are they interesting, they could also be dangerous!

VAMPIRE BATS: these bloodsuckers usually come out at night. They don't take enough blood to kill you, but they do spread diseases.

POISON DART FROGS: if you spot a brightly coloured frog, resist the temptation to pick it up – they are among the world's most poisonous creatures.

ELECTRIC EELS: lurking in murky rivers, these eels give a nasty shock if trodden on. People temporarily paralyzed by the shock have drowned as a result.

BULLET ANTS*: the size of your little finger, these ants are sometimes called the 24-hour ant – that's how long it takes for their sting to wear off. OW!

* Trivia: in some rainforest tribes, boys become men after wearing bullet-ant-filled gloves for 10 minutes – without crying.

ENVIRONMENT

Protest against a hydroelectric power plant that will flood a large area of rainforest

FOOTBALL

When you visit Brazil, you soon notice that nearly every bit of spare ground is being used by kids to play football. The sport is Brazil's national obsession. Brazil has the best record of any country in the World Cup, and there are Brazilian players in all the world's top leagues.

• •

FOOTBALL IN SÃO PAULO

Twenty million people live in São Paulo, Brazil's biggest city. The citizens are roughly divided between supporters of Sport Club Corinthians Paulista (commonly known as Corinthians), those who support São Paulo F.C and fans of Palmeiras. Matches between Corinthians and São Paulo are called Classico Majestoso – The Majestic Classic. These games, more than any other, are the ones each team is desperate to win.

By 2013, Corinthians were firmly on top, having won 116 of the 216 editions of the Classico. Corinthians also won the Brazilian title in 2011, and the South American and World club titles in 2012.

GREAT BRAZILIAN FOOTBALL RIVALRIES

PAULISTA DERBY

The Derby is Corinthians' bitter rivalry with another São Paulo club, Palmeiras, founded by former Corinthians in 1914. Corinthians fans are STILL smarting over the betrayal, 100 years later.

FLA-FLU

Two of Rio's most popular clubs, Flamengo and Fluminense, fight it out in the city's famous Maracanã Stadium. In 1963, 194,603 people watched the Fla-Flu – the biggest football crowd ever.

CLASSICO VOVÔ

Classico Vovô means 'Grandpa Classic': this match between two Rio clubs, Fluminense and Botafogo, is the oldest rivalry in Brazilian football. The first match between them was played in 1905 (Fluminense won 6–0).

WORLD CUP FOOTBALL

In 2014, the World Cup visits Brazil. Twelve cities host matches, spread across the country – being in any of these during June and July offers guaranteed football fever.

Manaus
(Arena Amazônia)

Fortaleza
(Castelão)

Natal
(Arena das Dunas)

Recife
(Arena Pernambuco)

Salvador
(Arena Fonte Nova)

Cuiaba
(Arena Pantanal)

Brasília
(Mané Garrincha)

Belo Horizonte
(Mineirão)

São Paulo
(Arena Corinthians)

Rio de Janeiro
(Maracanã)

Curitiba
(Arena da Baixada)

Porto Alegre
(Beira-Rio)

The host cities (with the locals' stadium names in brackets)

SPORT AND LEISURE

"In Brazil, every kid starts playing football very early. It's in our blood."

— Top Brazilian footballer Ronaldo

SOCIAL LIFE

Typical Brazilian family picnic

Brazilians love to socialise, especially with family and childhood friends. Whether it's just for lunch or a full-blown party, any excuse is good enough to get together. The music plays, people speak over each other and new dishes keep appearing from the kitchen.

FAMILY

The MOST important thing to Brazilians is their family. In Brazil, family isn't just parents, brothers and sisters. Brazilians think of uncles, aunts, grandparents, cousins, nephews and nieces as close family, too.

Few Brazilians want to live far from their families: down the street or round the corner is far enough. In the cities, apartment blocks often have several members of the same family living in different apartments. One family may take over a whole floor, or even the entire building.

FRIENDS

Friends come a close second to family. People make friends at school and go through the rest of their lives with the same friends. They get together regularly, especially to walk and chat in the evening, when the temperature is cooler and many street markets and cafés are busy.

BRAZILIANS AND THEIR NAMES

Most Brazilians have two surnames. The first comes from their grandfather on their mother's side, the second from their father. When a woman gets married, she usually drops her grandfather's name and replaces it with her husband's father's surname.

PARTY ETIQUETTE

Guests at someone's home or a party often bring a small gift. When visiting someone's home, it's thought polite to get there 30 minutes early. For a party, though, people will arrive an hour late or more.

THINGS TO TALK ABOUT...

Brazil! Brazilians often ask visitors what they think of the country. When you reply, remember that most Brazilians are very proud of their home.

Football is almost always a popular subject, as well as the beach and Brazil's improvements and successes as a country. (So, that's Brazil again...)

... AND SUBJECTS TO AVOID

Criticisms of Brazil: it's OK for Brazilians to criticise their own country, but not foreigners.

The rainforest, religion and wealth and poverty can all be tricky subjects. Questions about people's age or how much they earn are considered rude.

Coconut drinks on the beach

SPORT AND LEISURE

BEACH LIFE

Bonete Beach

British people say, 'That's up my street' to show that something is ideal. Brazilians say, *É minha praia* – 'That's my beach' – to mean the same thing. People here absolutely LOVE going to the beach. Any chance they get, most people pack up a bag with a towel, some suntan lotion and a swimming costume, and head off to one of the thousands of amazing beaches along Brazil's coastline.

TREKKING TO BONETE BEACH

Bonete is a beautiful beach in São Paulo state. It's very different from city beaches such as Copacabana. Bonete is great for intrepid explorers who are willing to carry their own food and shelter.

1. Getting to Bonete

The best way to get to the beach is to trek through the coastal rainforest. The path winds 15 km under trees and past waterfalls: by the time you arrive, you'll probably just want to run straight into the sea and cool off.

2. Settling in

Drying off, you'll find it easy to imagine how the coast here must have looked to the first arrivals from Portugal, hundreds of years ago. Set up camp for an overnight stay, and let your imagination go.

3. Heading for home

When you're ready to leave, if you don't want to repeat the walk in the opposite direction, you can catch a boat or canoe from the nearby fishermen's camp back up the river.

THE *BALNEÁRIO*

A balneário is more than just a beach: it's a beach resort, with cafés, entertainment, and often showers, toilets and lifeguards. All the facilities mean they can be unbearably crowded, or really lively, depending on your viewpoint!

INSIDER TIPS FOR TOP BEACHES

FERNANDO DE NORONHA:

this volcanic archipelago is 350 km off the coast of Brazil, and visitor numbers are strictly controlled. The beaches are great for snorkelling among the rich sea life.

FLORIANÓPOLIS:

with 42 beaches, there's something for most people here. The island is famous for its surf, and several of Brazil's biggest stars come from the area. Florianópolis is best known, though, for its music and party scene.

SALVADOR:

the lovely beaches in the capital city of Bahia are busy all year around and people come to visit them from all over Brazil. One of the main central Salvador beaches is Porto de Barra.

SPORT AND LEISURE

Fernando de Noronha

Florianópolis

MUSIC IN BRAZIL

Live performance at a nightclub

Everywhere you go in Brazil, you hear radios playing, guitars being strummed, drums, car stereos – music provides the background noise to daily life. While you hear familiar styles of music such as rock, hip-hop, and R&B, there's much more to Brazil's music scene.

TRADITIONAL RHYTHMS

'Traditional rhythms' sounds a bit old-person, but don't worry – these are rhythms you hear on the dance floors of New York, London and Sydney. Samba and bossa nova get played a lot, but the most popular style of music is *sertanejo*.

The *sertão*, from which this music gets its name, is remote countryside. Sertanejo acts normally feature two singers, usually men and often brothers. Traditionally the instruments were accordion and guitar. These days sertanejo *universitário*, using electronic instruments, is popular with younger people.

Sertanejo universitário singers

MUSIC FESTIVAL CALENDAR

These are three very different Brazilian music festivals:

MARCH
Lollapalooza Brazil (São Paulo):

This festival is heavy on the rock, with 2013 headliners including Pearl Jam, The Killers and The Black Eyed Peas.

MAY
Festival de Barreto (Pereira Barreto, São Paulo state):

This 3-day festival is a feast of MBP (see below) for lovers of one of Brazil's favourite types of music.

SEPTEMBER
Rock in Rio (Rio de Janeiro):

Should really be called 'All Kinds Of Music In Rio': you can hear lots of different big international acts here, not only rock. For Europeans, Rock in Rio also visits Portugal and Spain.

FUSION MUSIC

Brazil's fusion music blends together older styles and new instruments and rhythms. One of the most popular is MBP, which stands for *música popular Brasileira*. The singer Seu Jorge is a famous MBP musician – his album *The Life Aquatic Studio Sessions* is a good place to start to get a taste of MBP. Other fusion styles include Sambass, which fuses samba with drum & bass, axé, which fuses different African-Caribbean genres, and Brazilian 'funk', which is actually a local form of hip-hop.

Brazilian-funk-influenced British musician M.I.A. in action

MUSIC AND DANCE

SAMBA!

Samba is known around the world as the music of Brazil. It combines West African rhythms and dance steps with European instruments. Samba first developed in Rio, but is now popular throughout the country.

Samba school rehearsals

SAMBA BATTLES

The heart of Rio's carnival is a battle between the city's 200 or so samba schools. Each school's entry involves elaborate costumes, highly decorated floats (as many as eight per school), specially written songs and up to 4,000 people.

A dance school parades at the Rio Carnival

LEARNING TO SAMBA

Many Brazilians start dancing samba not long after they learned to walk, so they make it look REALLY simple. And the basic step for samba IS simple. It's a backward-and-forward step, done with loose hips and bent knees. But the rhythm of samba is quite fast and things get complicated pretty quickly – especially if you're trying to keep up with a Brazilian. The best way to learn samba is to attend a class. There are dance schools all over Brazil, but in Rio, the samba heartland, it is especially easy to find a class.

SAMBA ART?

Samba is associated with a style of painting called 'naïve art'. The bright colours and countryside scenes have a very Brazilian feel. There's a Museum of Naïve Art of Brazil in Cosme Velho, Rio de Janeiro state.

"Samba music [has] layers of separate rhythms that overlap and create a hot, bumpin' tapestry of sound."

— Samba dancer and teacher, Theresa Stevens

DANCE IN BRAZIL

Samba isn't the only Brazilian dance style. Here are three more:

FORRÓ:

originally from northeastern Brazil, forró is danced by a couple, holding each other close. It can be slow, medium or fast-paced.

LAMBADA:

in the northeast of Brazil, lambada developed from *carimbó*, a dance so suggestive it was once known as 'the forbidden dance'. The dancers sway their hips from side-to-side, and dramatic spins are common.

ZOUK:

zouk just means 'party' in the Caribbean, where this dance originated. It was bound to be popular in Brazil, where it blended with lambada to form *Lambada-Zouk!*

FESTIVALS **IN BRAZIL**

Bumba meu boi oxen

In a country that loves a party as much as Brazil, there's no shortage of fabulous festivals to check out. The biggest is carnival (see pages 40-41), but there are some less well-known festivals that are a real treat for travellers.

Festas Juninas

SÃO LUÍS: **BUMBA MEU BOI**
(July–August)

At the heart of the massive party of Bumba meu boi is a crazy tale about an ox that is killed and eaten, then brought back to life. The story is told and re-told by street performers dressed as oxen or mythical creatures. The crowd joins in, heckling and encouraging the artists.

PARATY: **CORPUS CHRISTI** FESTIVAL
(usually in June)

The streets of this traditional seaside town are covered in 'carpets': really patterns of sawdust, leaves, flowers, chalk and coffee grounds. The religious procession walks over the carpet, after which it is ruined.

CAMPINA GRANDE: *FESTAS JUNINAS*
(June)

The *Festas Juninas* are celebrations of Brazil's traditional countryside way of life. They happen throughout the country, but Campinha Grande holds one of the biggest. People dress in the check shirts and straw hats of rural workers. They dance to forró music of accordions and triangles, and eat *canjica*, a kind of porridge.

> "I dream all year of this day... This is always a sacred occasion for me, full of hope and joy."
>
> — Rosilene Gouveia Aguiar, one of the crowd at the *Círio de Nazaré* festival

BELÉM: *CÍRIO DE NAZARÉ*
(October)

This festival honours the statue of Our Lady of Nazareth, which lives in a church at Belém. The statue is said to have performed miracles, including mysteriously moving itself from the town to the riverbank nearby. The statue is pulled on a cart to the river, then hundreds of boats escort it to Icoaraci and back.

Our Lady of Nazareth takes to the water, Belém

PUBLIC HOLIDAYS

These are the major public holidays in Brazil, but there are other regional holidays as well.

DATE:	HOLIDAY:
1 January	New Year's Day
21 April	Tiradentes Day, celebrating a campaigner for Brazilian independence
1 May	Labour Day
7 September	Independence Day
12 October	Our Lady of Aparecida
2 November	All Souls Day
15 November	Republic Day
25 December	Christmas Day/ *Noël*

CARNIVAL!

Most Brazilians are Roman Catholics. In the days before Easter, they celebrate Lent, giving up luxurious foods and eating smaller meals. To let off steam before Lent, people celebrate carnival – a massive party that's impossible to miss if you're visiting Brazil.

Height of the carnival at the Sambodromo, Rio de Janeiro

BRAZIL'S BEST CARNIVALS

Where should you head to experience Brazilian carnival at its best? The Rio Carnival is probably the BIGGEST – over two million people are said to hit the streets every day for the celebrations. But plenty of Brazilians will tell you that there are other carnivals around the country just as good – or even better:

SALVADOR (Bahia state)

For a week, the streets are patrolled

by the *trios eléctricos*, trucks carrying bands playing LOUD music – all night. Every year there's a different theme, and the whole city is decorated accordingly.

OLINDA (Pernambuco state)

Carnival here is an amazing, very Brazilian mixture of cultures. Olinda is one of Brazil's best-preserved Portuguese-colonial cities. The carnival here is similar to traditional Portuguese versions, but with the addition of African-style music and dances.

PORTO SEGURO
(Bahia state)

The focus of the celebrations is the city's famous *Passarela do Álcool*, one of the main streets through town. *Trios eléctricos* and *cordões* (processions of dancers) drag the party down the Passarela and to the beach. (Another highlight of this area is the beautiful white sandy beaches.)

GET WITH THE *BANDA*...

In Rio, away from the main parade there are also street parties in most neighbourhoods. The big ones feature *bandas*, semi-organised parades led by bands of wandering musicians, which anyone can join.

... BUT NOT WITH THE *BLOCO*

At many carnivals, the dancers follow carnival floats in *blocos*, semi-organised groups of people. Each bloco is usually surrounded by a rope. You can't duck under the rope unless you're part of the bloco!

Carnival crowds at Olinda

Ivete Sangalo, famous trio electrico in Porto Seguro

FESTIVALS IN BRAZIL

KEY INFORMATION
FOR TRAVELLERS

LANGUAGE

Portuguese is spoken throughout Brazil, though with a different accent from people who come from Portugal. Learning a few words will always get a good reaction from Brazilians, but English is also spoken in many tourist areas.

ENTERING BRAZIL

Your passport must be valid for at least six months after your arrival in Brazil, or you won't be allowed in. EU citizens do not need a visa, but people from most other places (including Australia, Canada and the USA) do.

While in Brazil, everyone is required to carry proof of identity, at all times. A photocopy of the relevant page of your passport should be OK – but check before you go for the latest information.

GETTING AROUND

Brazil is a huge country, and much of it is rough countryside or thick forest. Railways are generally not a good way to get around. Roads can sometimes be excellent, but others are poor quality, which makes travelling long distances by car time-consuming and tiring. As a result, many people make long journeys between cities by plane. An alternative if travelling along the coast or along rivers is to take a ferry: slower, but more relaxing and fun.

Within cities and towns, buses are a good way to get around, and both Rio and São Paulo have metro train systems. Cycling is not that common in Brazil: bikes are mainly used by people who can't afford a motor vehicle. Cities such as São Paulo are trying to encourage cycling, as a way of increasing fitness and cutting traffic, but hiring a bike isn't really recommended for visitors.

PERIGO
Área sujeita a ataque de tubarão

DANGER
Bathers in this area are at a greater Than average risk of shark attack

Surfing has been banned at some Pernambuco beaches because of shark attacks

HEALTH

Several serious diseases can be caught in Brazil, including malaria, yellow fever, bilharzia and dengue fever. It's best to drink only bottled water, and make sure food is well cooked, or washed and peeled if raw.

If you are unlucky enough to get ill, healthcare is very good in towns and cities. It is expensive, though, and Brazil does not have agreements with other countries to treat their citizens for free. Travel insurance is essential.

POSTAL SERVICES

The national post service is called *Correios*, which is Portuguese for 'post'. Letters and parcels take anything from a day to a week to arrive within Brazil, while airmail takes about a week to reach foreign countries.

MOBILE NETWORKS

Mobile coverage is good in most towns and cities, but in rural and isolated areas there may be no coverage at all. Using a foreign phone – even on the same network – is expensive, especially for data, so it's important to turn off data roaming. You can buy SIMs easily, and top-ups (*cartoes pre-pago*) for Brazilian SIM cards are available at newspaper kiosks.

INTERNET PROVISION

In bigger cities, Internet access is generally good. There are Internet cafés in most towns, cities and tourist hotspots, and Wifi is available in many hotels. In rural areas coverage is less reliable, but in smaller towns there may be public Internet access at post offices.

STAYING SAFE

Brazil can be a dangerous place for travellers, particularly cities such as Rio de Janeiro and São Paulo. Crimes such as robbery are not uncommon. Minimise the risks:

- Never wear expensive watches or jewellery in public

- Avoid going out in expensive designer-label clothes or shoes, or letting people see you have high-cost electronic goods

- Only carry as much money as you need, and try to avoid carrying large amounts

- Never accept lifts from people you do not know and always be wary of situations where you may find yourself alone with strangers

- If you take a taxi, check that it is officially licensed

THE ESSENTIALS

CURRENCY:

Brazilian real, symbol BRL or R$ (R$1 = roughly £0.33, €0.38, or US$0.50). Currency exchange at banks, *cambios* and some hotels. ATM cash withdrawal is possible in towns and cities.

TELEPHONE DIALLING CODES:

To call Brazil from outside the country, add the exit code from your country (from the UK this is OO), add 55 to the beginning of the number, and drop the zero from the city code.

To call another country from Brazil, add oo and the country code of the place you are dialling to the beginning of the number, and drop the zero.

*Cartões telefônico*s, pre-paid telephone cards, can be bought at newspaper kiosks and used in public phones.

TIME ZONE:

There are three time zones in Brazil:

Brasilia Time, which is 3 hours behind GMT

Amazon Standard Time, which is 4 hours behind GMT

Fernando de Noronha Archipelago Time, which is 2 hours behind GMT

OPENING HOURS:

Opening hours tend to be different in the city from the countryside, and in different parts of Brazil. As a rough guide, most shops open at between 08:00 and 09:00, and shut for the day at about 22:00. On Sundays opening hours are shorter.

USEFUL WORDS AND PHRASES:
Portuguese pronunciation can be trick but it's still worth trying to learn a few words and phrases before visiting Brazil:

Desculpe, eu não falo português	Sorry, I don't speak Portuguese
Sim/não	Yes/no
obrigado/obrigada	Thank you (spoken by a man/woman)
Tudo bem?	How's it going? (This is a friendly greeting: the response is also *Tudo bem*)
Legal	Cool. (Just as slippery a word in Brazilian Portuguese as 'cool' is in English. People, clothes music, statements and plans can all be *legal*.)
O Brasil é lindo maravilhoso!	Brazil is magnificent! (All Brazilians will approve.)

FINDING OUT MORE

BOOKS TO READ: NON-FICTION

Countries in Our World: *Brazil:*
Edward Parker (Franklin Watts, 2012)
Informative, fact-packed guide to Brazil.
It includes physical features, daily life,
industry, media, leisure and much more.

Rio de Janeiro: Simon Scoones (Evans
Brothers, 2006)
Zooming in on the city that attracts
more visitors to Brazil than any other,
this book contains information on how
the city is changing, its neighbourhoods,
environmental concerns, and much more.

BOOKS TO READ: FICTION

Journey to the River Sea: *Eva* Ibbotson
(Macmillan, 2001)
This book was shortlisted for many
major writing prizes. It tells the story
of Maia Fielding, an orphan who travels
to Manaus in the Brazilian Amazon
from the UK to live with her relatives,
the Carters. There she gets involved
in a complicated plot involving child
actors, the heir to a grand estate,
Indian tribes and much, much more.

The Summer Prince: Alaya Dawn
Johnson (Arthur A Levine Books, 2013)
Years in the future, in the Brazilian city
of Palmares Três, June Costa meets
Enki. They fall in love – but Enki is to be
the Summer King, and in a city ruled by
women, this means he's doomed to die…

WEBSITES

http://www.visitbrasil.com
This is the official tourist guide to Brazil,
and is packed with useful information.
At the bottom of the page are the most
useful tabs, buttons that lead to sections
on tips for travellers, information about
the country and its regions, and popular
destinations. You can also download
'Brasil Quest', a game in which you
navigate the character Yep to the 12 host
cities for the 2014 World Cup.

http://www.brazil.org.za
This site is packed with information about
Brazil, including its states and cities, the
country's culture, sports, landscapes and
animals. Just use the pull-down menus
from the top of the page to find whatever
you're interested in.

**https://www.cia.gov/library/
publications/the-world-factbook/
geos/br.html**
This link will take you to the CIA (Central
Intelligence Agency) web page about
Brazil. It's quite dry, but crammed full of
useful information and statistics.

Note to parents and teachers:
Every effort has been made by the Publishers
to ensure that these websites are suitable
for children, that they are of the highest
educational value, and that they contain no
inappropriate or offensive material. However,
because of the nature of the Internet, it is
impossible to guarantee that the contents of
these sites will not be altered. We strongly
advise that Internet access is supervised by a
responsible adult.

THE ESSENTIALS

INDEX